APOSTLES LUTHERAN CHURCH
5828 SANTA TERESA BLVD.
SAN JOSE, CA 95123

Mom's Pregnant

Darlene Hoffa

Illustrated by Rick Incrocci

To Christopher and Melissa and Danielle —
our three miracles.

Copyright © 1997 by Educational Publishing Concepts, Inc., Wheaton, Illinois

Published by Concordia Publishing House
3558 S. Jefferson Avenue, St. Louis, MO 63118-3968
Manufactured in the United States of America

1 2 3 4 5 6 7 8 9 10   06 05 04 03 02 01 00 99 98 97

Mom's pregnant!
Let's laugh and sing!
Let's tell friends the news!
Let's learn how a baby comes to be.

One special day, Mom and Dad join together to have a child. Soon, Dad's tiny-tiny sperm enters Mom's tiny egg. The egg and sperm unite. They make one cell that is smaller than this dot . ! At this moment a new life begins. In nine months, this cell will grow to be a baby.

God, our Father who created us, knows all about this baby. He wrote the baby's design inside the single cell. He wrote with coded messages called genes. Genes decide if the baby will have Dad's dark hair or Mom's bouncy curls, Mom's slim body or Dad's strong build.

fun to do: Decide whom you look like in your family.

About twelve hours after it is formed, the little cell divides into two cells. These cells divide again. All the cells keep dividing about twice a day.

The cells drift toward Mom's uterus. The uterus is a place in Mom's body that God created for making babies. The cluster of cells burrows snugly into the soft uterus lining. At first, baby is called an *embryo*.

fun to do: Find the place in the picture where the baby grows in Mom.

The cells keep dividing. In one week, the embryo grows to more than a hundred cells. The embryo is still smaller than the head of a pin! But don't let the tiny size fool you. God is doing a miracle!

The cells keep dividing into more and more cells. God tells each cell what part of the baby to make. Some cells become brain cells. Some become bone cells. Some become heart cells. An embryo needs many kinds of cells to become a baby.

fun to do: Name other parts of the baby the embryo needs to make.

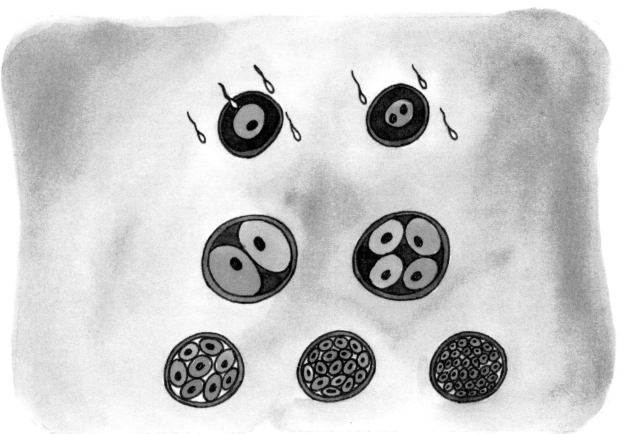

The embryo doesn't look like a baby yet. But God will change the top of the embryo into baby's face and neck. The "tail" at the bottom of the embryo keeps the baby's early spinal cord safe.

The embryo is so small—half the size of a green pea, just one-fourth of an inch long. Still, buds pop out where arms and legs will grow. The brain and digestive system start to form. *Beat, beat, beat* pounds the tiny heart.

fun to do: See how long one-fourth of an inch is on a ruler. Find things that tiny in your house. Then give Mom a hug.

During the second month the embryo begins to look like a tiny baby. A face begins to form. The brain keeps developing. The bones get more solid. The organs are in place. Little arms no longer than a printed exclamation mark (!) have tiny hands with fingers and thumbs. The slower growing legs have knees and ankles and feet with toes.

By the end of two months, the embryo is about the size of a large lime. God still has lots of work to do, but every part baby needs to become an adult is formed. Now we call the baby a *fetus*.

fun to do:

Mom's tummy may feel upset. Get some crackers for her.

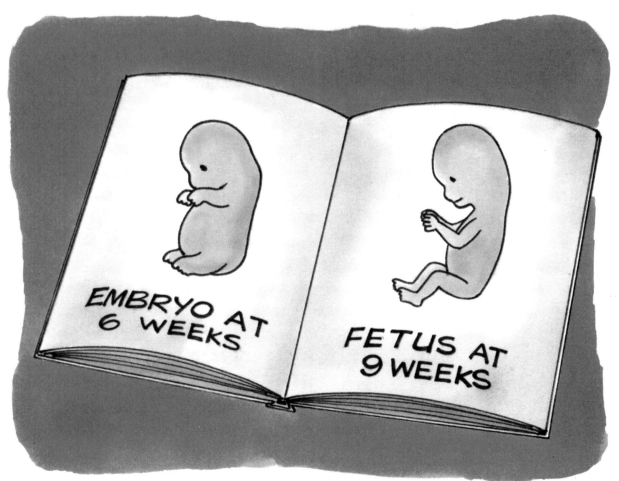

EMBRYO AT 6 WEEKS

FETUS AT 9 WEEKS

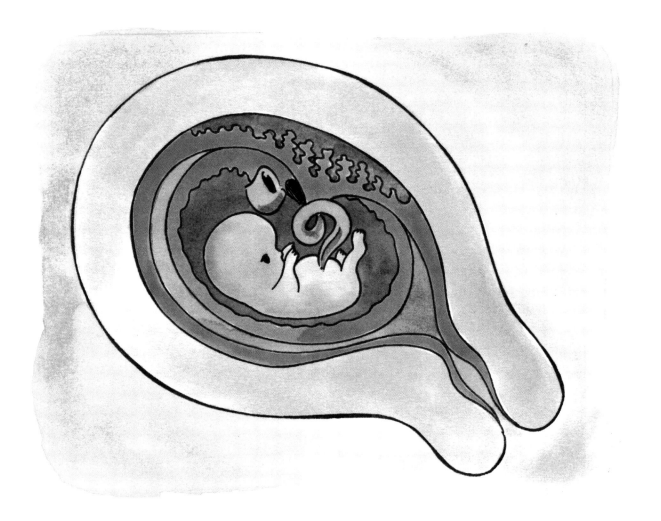

Inside Mom's uterus, baby lives like a little astronaut in a space capsule. He moves freely inside a water-filled sac, as if weightless in space. This bubble of water protects baby from bumps as Mom moves around.

Baby's umbilical cord works like an astronaut's lifeline. The cord connects him to the placenta. The placenta works like an astronaut's life support. It gives the baby nourishment and air and removes waste. God thinks of everything!

fun to do:
Name some ways your baby is like an astronaut.

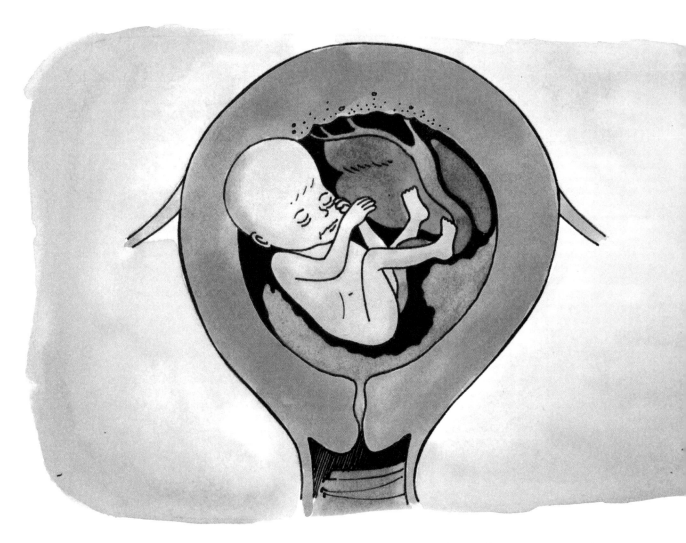

If you could peek at baby during the third month,
you'd see: A face that looks more like your face. A mouth
opening and closing. Arms and hands moving. Legs
kicking. Signs of fingernails and toenails. And eyelids shut

tightly like a baby kitten's. And you could tell if your baby is your new brother or sister!

fun to do: Mom may like strange combinations of food now. Help Dad fix her a snack.

At four months, baby measures eight to ten inches long and weighs about six ounces. He may suck his thumb and swallow. He might recognize your voice. He has his own fingerprints and footprints. You can look at your baby with an ultrasound picture.

Flutter, flutter. Mom feels movement inside her like butterfly wings. As baby grows bigger and stronger, Mom feels: *Loopity loop! Kick! Punch! Dive!* Baby romps joyfully in his watery home.

fun to do: Visit an ultrasound lab. Talk and sing to your baby every day.

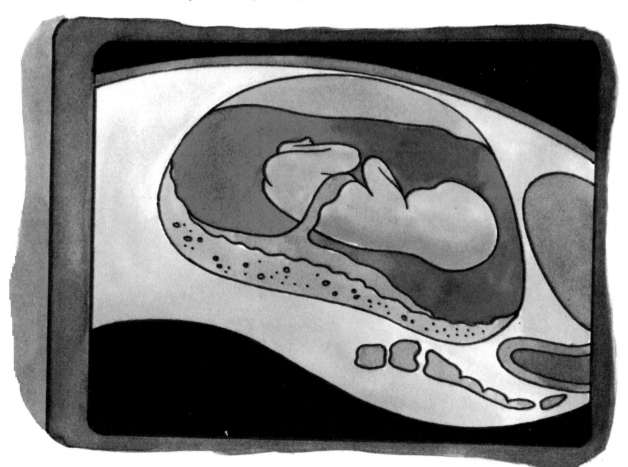

At five months, baby is about the size of a small doll. He has a fringe of eyelashes and delicate eyebrows. You might be able to hear his fast heartbeat through Mom's tummy. *Beat! Beat! Beat!*

Baby chooses a favorite position to sleep, just like you do. He wakes and naps. He hiccups too. Noises make him jump, as if he is asking, "What's going on out there?"

fun to do: Try to listen to your baby's heartbeat.

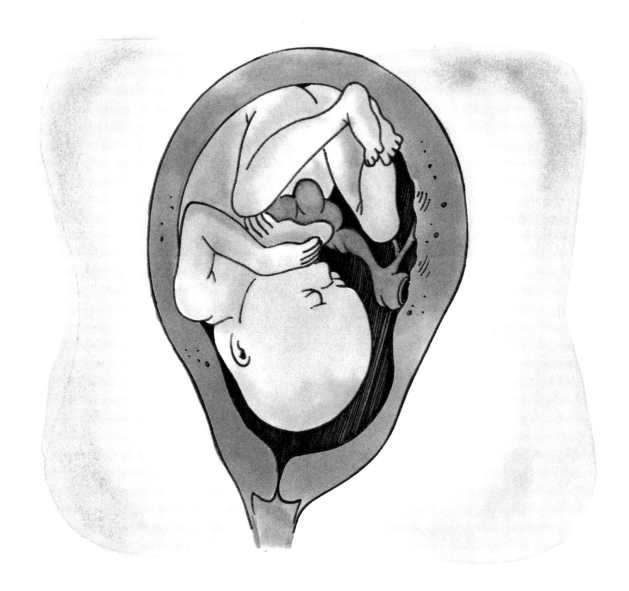

At six months, baby looks red and wrinkly. He needs fat under his skin to make it smoother. He measures about fifteen inches long and weighs over two pounds.

Baby's eyes open now. They look up, look down, and they look side to side. Soon they will see God's beautiful world!

fun to do: Take walks with Mom. Be a happy helper.

At seven months, baby weighs about three-and-a-half pounds. His once roomy home feels cramped. He trades cartwheels for stretches and thumb-sucking.

During the eighth month, God pads a cuddly layer of fat under baby's skin. Baby can see. His lungs and digestive tract are almost complete. Each day spent inside Mom, with the placenta's air and food supply, makes baby stronger. He probably settles head-down to await birth.

fun to do: Mom feels big and uncomfortable now. Help her slip on her shoes. Bring her a pillow.

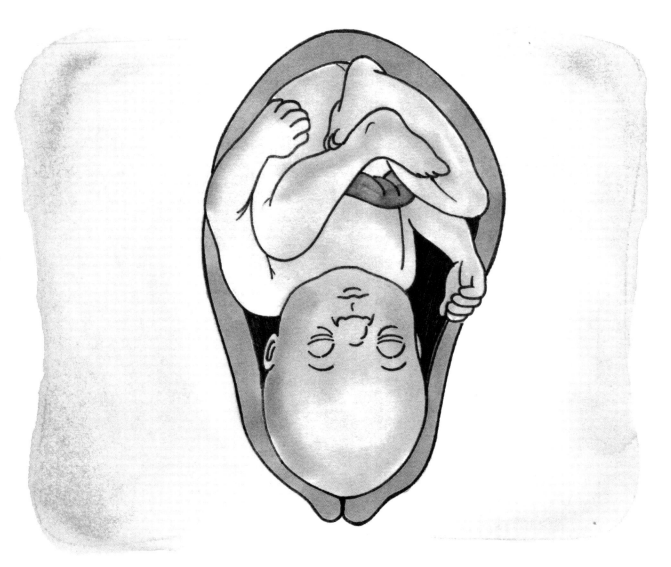

During the final weeks, God delivers antibodies from Mom's blood to baby. These antibodies will keep baby from getting certain illnesses, if Mom has had them. The heavy uterus, filled with the growing baby, sinks lower in Mom's body.

The ninth and last month arrives. If average size, the baby weighs about seven-and-a-half pounds and measures twenty-one inches long. His lungs mature. He prepares for the great adventure of birth. *S-t-r-e-t-c-h, s-t-r-e-t-c-h.* You can feel bulges on Mom's tummy as baby stretches.

fun to do:

Visit the place where your baby will be born. What will you do during the baby's birth?

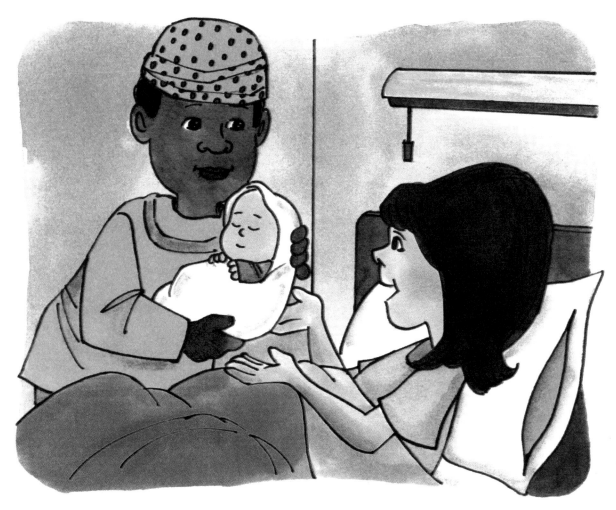

Finally, Mom's body knows. It's time for the baby to be born. Mom and Dad call the doctor. The uterus slowly contracts to push baby out. With its job done, the bubble of water breaks. Down, down the birth canal baby moves. Baby's head comes out. *Whoosh!* Here comes the rest of him!

"Wa-a-a!" baby cries. His lungs work hard to fill with air for the first time. The doctor cuts baby's umbilical cord and delivers the placenta. Baby can breathe and eat without their help now. Baby snuggles in Mom's arms and looks for his first meal.

fun to do:
Make a sign to welcome your new brother or sister.

"Hooray!" you shout with Mom and Dad. "We have a brand-new person to love." From one cell, God has made your beautiful baby, the same way He made you.

"Oh, thank You, God!" you say. "A baby is Your best miracle of all."

fun to do:

Ask Mom and Dad about the day you were born. Look at pictures taken of you on your birth day.

Dear Parent:

Use this book to prepare your child for the birth of a new brother or sister. Simplify the text and terms, when necessary, so they are appropriate for your child. With a very young child, you may just want to discuss the pictures and do the activities. Or you may want to talk about one or two pages in the book each month, as your pregnancy develops.

Involve your child in helping you prepare for the baby. Look at your child's own baby pictures and talk about how he or she has grown. Above all, thank God often for the gift of life. As a family, plan how you will share God's love with your baby. Pray often that you will have a healthy baby who will love Jesus as you do.

APOSTLES LUTHERAN CHURCH
5828 SANTA TERESA BLVD.
SAN JOSE, CA 95123